How to Have It All

How to Have It All

The Secrets of the Proverbs 31 Woman

BY IMANI ACKERMAN

Dedications

To Madre Mia & Daddy
I love you. (Mom, you're next!)

To Keeks and Teesh, my besties
Thank you for encouraging my crazy!

To Mama L
You're the best.

To my beloved, Roddy
Thank you for believing in me.

To Princess Z and the ones to come,
I promise to model for you what this book is all about.

Above all, thank you, Jesus!

Table of Contents

Part I — The Story

Proverbs 31:10-31 TLV, emphasis mine

A Woman of Valor
10 An **accomplished woman** who can find?
Her value is far beyond rubies.
11 Her husband's heart **trusts** in her,
and he lacks nothing valuable.
12 She **brings him good** and not harm
all the days of her life.
13 She **selects** wool and flax
and her hands work willingly.
14 She **is like** merchant ships,
bringing her sustenance from afar.
15 She **rises** while it is still night
and provides food for her household
and portions for her servant girls.
16 She **considers** a field and buys it.
From the fruit of her hands she plants a vineyard.
17 She **girds** herself with strength
and invigorates her arms.
18 She **discerns** that her business is good.
Her lamp never goes out at night.
19 She **extends** her hands to the spindle
and her palm **grasps** the spinning wheel.
20 She **spreads** out her palms to the poor,
and **extends** her hands to the needy.
21 She is **not afraid** of snow for her house,
for her whole household is clothed in scarlet wool.

22 She makes her own luxurious **coverings**.
Her clothing is fine linen and purple.
23 Her husband is **respected** at the city gates,
when he sits among the elders of the land.
24 She makes **linen** garments and sells them
and supplies sashes to the merchants.
25 **Strength and dignity** are her clothing,
and she laughs at the days to come.
26 She opens her **mouth** with wisdom—
a lesson of kindness is on her tongue.
27 She **watches** over the affairs of her household,
and does not eat the bread of idleness.
28 Her children **arise** and bless her,
her husband also praises her:
29 "**Many** daughters have excelled,
but you surpass them all."
30 Charm is **deceitful** and beauty is vain,
but a woman who fears *Adonai* will be praised.
31 **Give** her the fruit of her hands.
Let her deeds be her praise at the gates.

2

Introduction

I absolutely love The Wiz. The Wiz is an urban twist on The Wizard of Oz. I have never read the book and the Broadway play wasn't running during my lifetime, but since Michael Jackson plays the Scarecrow in the movie and he's my all-time favorite entertainer, naturally I love the movie. The Wiz has a mostly Black cast of characters so it is an historically significant work. The music for the movie was produced by Quincy Jones. Diana Ross played Dorothy. Critics — whoever they were — thought the movie was just "okay." How?! I don't know what weird Koolaid they were drinking — I think everything about The Wiz is epic! That's why my family watches it every Thanksgiving and then some.

In case you don't know, the Wiz is about a 25-year-old woman named Dorothy who is afraid to leave her Harlem home, and her Auntie Em and Uncle Henry who raised her. Then, one evening, after Thanksgiving dinner, her dog, Toto, runs out of the house into a blizzard. Dorothy chases after him and gets caught in a swirl of snow that takes her to the land of Oz. From there she has to figure out how to get back home. With newfound silver slippers on her feet and an entourage of friends, who are also on a quest for self-discovery, Dorothy seeks out the

Wiz who will help her get home. The journey is perilous — there is a witch trying to kill her along the way — but she prevails in the end.

The Wiz and The Wizard of Oz are similar in plot except for this: when Diana Ross' Dorothy finally arrives with her friends to Emerald City, where the Wiz lives, she realizes he is a fake. He's a regular guy from New Jersey who is really good at making people believe he's powerful. He can't do anything for her. It breaks Dorothy's heart and discourages her friends that they'll never become who they want to be.

That's when Dorothy reminds her friends that they already had what they wanted. The journey helped them to become who they wanted to be. And because she knew her mind, heart, and courage, all she needed to do to get home was to believe in herself and click her silver heels three times. A song feature from the world-class Lena Horne, who plays Glinda the Good Witch, makes me teary-eyed every time — and I'm not ashamed to say it! "Believe in yourself as I believe in you," she sings.

I say all of this not just to pay homage to this seemingly little-known classic, but to give you a heads up: this book is going to reveal, as Judy Garland's Wizard of Oz said, "the man behind the curtain," — in reference to the identity of the

Wizard. Except, in the case of this book, the "man behind the curtain" is a woman.

I titled this book *How to Have It All*, because I, like many Christian women, have wondered whether it was possible to be a strong woman of God, wife, mother, ministry leader, entrepreneur, writer, artist, etc. In my decade-long faith journey I continually discover that nothing is impossible with God. And even now, I have it all!

Oftentimes, Christian women have looked to the Bible, as we should, to see how we can become who God has called us to be, and that includes looking to the Book of Proverbs, chapter 31. Unfortunately, we often take this chapter out of context, creating impossible standards for women of modern times. The woman mentioned in the chapter can seemingly do it "all" — she's Martha Stewart + Beyonce + Oprah with more kids than Angelina Jolie and a husband who rivals Barack Obama in admiration. And she loves God!

We often read Proverbs 31 as a tribute to a woman's life accomplishments or, worse, as a snapshot or a "day-in-the-life." We use her as a checklist, often to the detriment of our self-esteem and self-worth. We see our inadequacies, our shortcomings, our skill deficits, and then we see the Proverbs 31 woman. We either obsess over how to mirror her, hoping that, if we embody a few of the verses, we can "have it all," or we reject all possibilities of becoming like her.

Here is where The Wiz analogy comes back around. It's as if we, like Dorothy, are looking outwardly for something that can help us become the women we want to be. We think that if we do the things she did that would make us like her. Doing what she did would fix us. Aspiring to be like her would change us. For those of us who call ourselves Christians, this is not only wrong thinking, it's blasphemous. It's completely contrary to the Gospel of Jesus.

But God put The Proverbs 31 woman in Scripture for a reason. She shows us that in and through Jesus we can "have it all." Looking to her story is not in vain, but I can almost guarantee that you've been reading it the wrong way. The key is to know the *entire* story, and read it in the right context. So that's what we are going to do. I am going to show you the secrets of The Proverbs 31 Woman, what and how we can learn from her, and how to put those things into practice, to the glory of God.

To be completely honest, I think you're going to be mad at me after reading this book. It'll be the good kind of mad, though. You are going to realize that The Proverbs 31 Woman is a lot like the Wiz. Lack of scholarship and teaching about her over time has perpetuated this narrative of the "great and powerful" woman, and you may find that your version of her is a fake. The difference between the Wiz and The Proverbs 31 Woman is that the Wiz teaches Dorothy from his failures, and The Proverbs 31 Woman teaches us from her success. More so, The Proverbs 31 Woman has success that is rooted in biblical principles. And, the good news is, as you study God's Word to discover who she is and who God has made you to be, you absolutely will learn How to Have It All.

I think "having it all" is a requirement for women of God. Yes, I think it is a must. When we are thriving, regardless of circumstances and seasons, we are living in God's will and everybody benefits. I thoroughly intend to mess up your idea of who The Proverbs 31 woman is by helping you see the truth in Scripture. In doing so, I hope to set you up to pursue God and see your dreams and desires come to fruition for His glory, to bless the world.

Chapter 1

I can't recall where I was or exactly how old I was when I read Proverbs 31, but I remember being no older than a young teenager and feeling frustrated that in order to be a "wife of noble character" I had to be married and a full-time homemaker. Reading my English translation of the Bible was discouraging, and resources guiding me to learn to sew and how to dress seemed to go against how I am wired. (I don't like being told what to do if I don't know why that's the best practice. That's the difference between being religious and having an authentic relationship with God. Yes, I take Him at His word, but I also try to understand His heart.) Not that I don't love sewing, but I couldn't find the balance between my desire to be a professional and leader, and old theologians pretty much insisting that I adopt an Amish lifestyle.

Disappointingly, as I've read commentaries about Proverbs 31, there's not a lot about how this Scripture applies to our lives today, and much of the advice that does exist is antiquated. I find that the commentaries I've read have been written mostly by men and some of them insist that this proverb is about a woman who knew how to manage her home. For real? That's all you got, guys? While that is part of the accomplishments listed in that passage of scripture, some commentaries seem to deny that the Proverbs 31 Woman was also a business woman. They deny that she had it "all."

These days "having it all" refers to having a top-level career and having a family. Of course not everyone wants that so "having it all" varies from person to person. However, I don't believe men have to ask the question of whether they can have it all as much as women do. Women are constantly pressured to choose between our careers and our families. More so, in some subcultures of Christianity, we sometimes have this subtle idea that a woman choosing her career "over" her family, or at least choosing to invest in her career while having young kids, is selfish. Sometimes we make it seem like being a mother is the highest calling a woman could have — as if "callings" can be ranked in order of significance and single women with no children couldn't possibly be as effective for the glory of God as mothers could. To be clear, this is a lie. In fact, the Apostle Paul even encouraged men and women to remain single if possible (1 Corinthians 7:6-8). A whole book could be written about why God allowed Paul's opinion about singleness and marriage to be part of our Bibles. At the same time, I do agree, wholeheartedly, with the Andy Stanley quote, " Your greatest contribution to the kingdom of God may not be something you do but someone you raise." However, I know that

Stanley was speaking to men as well as women; grandparents, teachers, pastors, and community leaders as well as parents. Raising the next generation is indeed a high calling, and though that may include our own children, that is not limited to the home.

As a matter of fact, being a woman who wears multiple hats is one of the greatest gifts we can give to the young people in our lives. When we use our talents and skills and personalities to make a difference in our world, whether by working outside of or from the home, volunteering, serving at church, or leading a homeschooling group, we are also being an example of what they can do when they use all of what God has given them, much like the Proverbs 31 woman is an example to us.

I'm a millennial. I was raised to believe that I could do anything. My generation is the "you're special" generation. My mother is a Jamaican immigrant and my father is a Guyanese immigrant. Both are scholars who worked hard to create the careers and reputations they have today. My dad is a retired educator who impacted the lives of students as a teacher and dean at a New York City private school. He has had an active lifestyle over the years, taking up backpacking and cross-city biking as hobbies, and he has also written tons of poetry and taken up photography. He is now a published author, philanthropist (including a kidney donation to a co-worker he barely knew), and grandpa. When my mom came to the U.S. she had a teaching degree and a Bachelors in Theology, but her first job here was working on an ice cream truck. My mom earned her Masters in Special Education while my little sister and I were young kids. She worked with adults for several years before becoming a teacher. She is also writing a book and launching a new ministry at her church. I have heard my mom lament that she was not able to breastfeed my sister as long as she wanted because she had to go back to work, but we never felt like we were missing out.

Somehow my parents managed to keep our house clean, grow in their careers, create incredible memories for us, and encourage us in our academic and personal development. Whenever I had a dream or passion, my parents fanned the flame. I wanted to be the first African-American female president of the United States and I was reading books on the subject in 2nd grade! I wanted to be a dancer, so I took dance and choreography classes. I wanted to be an entrepreneur like Madame C.J. Walker — my parents took me to get my babysitter's certification at the American Red Cross at 11 years old, which came in handy when I started babysitting at 14.

My parents have built a legacy and continue to model for me what can be accomplished when you put your mind to it. When I became a Christian at 16, I had even bigger dreams — God-sized dreams.

I knew I was chosen by God to do things for Him in His Kingdom, as we all are. I was passionate about making a difference in the lives of others, especially through ministry, compassion, community, and using my talents. But there was an underlying unspoken message that I saw in ministry: when a woman gets married and has kids, your career goes on the back burner. That's what good Christian women do. I soon put my dreams on the back burner as well.

That should've never happened. I was the first Black female pastor at the church where I became a Christian, and the youngest pastor in the history of that church — 21 years old. My midwestern middle-aged, White, male pastor and boss was thrilled to have me on staff as the Student Ministries pastor. I was dating my husband, Roddy, at the time who was not a credentialed minister. When praying about the longevity of our romantic relationship, I told God, "I really like Roddy, but I know I'm called to do a lot of 'big things.' I don't want to have to lay down what you're calling me to do in order to be his wife, and I hope he doesn't expect that from me. So, Jesus, please work that out." Roddy and I never had a conversation about it before marriage, but his obvious support for me, as I walked into that ministry role with a flashier "title" than his, making more money on paper than he did, proved what I knew when I married him: he was not intimidated by a "strong" woman with a "bold" calling to be a leader. He would never require that I hide in his shadow. A note of encouragement for my single friends who desire to be wives someday: wait for the man who won't make you play small.

Fast-forward a few years and one daughter later, suddenly, I was an unemployed stay-at-home mom and Roddy was the youth pastor at a different church. Staying home was partly a financial decision and partly a decision to wait until my daughter was a bit older to put her in childcare. I was burned out and had no desire to do ministry so I chose to hide in Roddy's shadow. It was my choice. I didn't realize then how much I would resent being there. It was not where God called me to be, but I, like many moms, became the martyr of the family. I thought, "This is what women are called to do." I even had other women counsel me to wait until my daughter was a bit older to pursue the dreams God gave me. They simultaneously encouraged me to find my "place." I felt so lost and confused.

So often Christian women take the religious interpretations of commentaries and counselors instead of walking in the freedom God gave us when we started our relationships with Him. We assume that just because the well-meaning Christian culture around us believes a certain thing about the way we are "supposed" to live our lives, we should make that our truth as well. This happens most

14

easily when we don't believe in ourselves. When we don't believe we have anything to offer. When we're tired. When we're in transition. When we're just over it and don't want to fight anymore. Getting back to that place where we fully live as who God made us to be — not who people think God made us to be — can be difficult, but it's possible and worth it.

That being said, when Bible scholars and teachers basically remove huge chunks of The Proverbs 31 Woman's story as if she was only a wife and mom who just happened to make a little extra money on the side, it drives me nuts. Actually, it pisses me off. For one, it's an inaccurate reading of the Word, and you don't need a Bible degree to figure that out. The Proverbs 31 Woman was not only able to raise her family and keep a home (with the help of servants, thank you very much), she ran multiple businesses, namely real estate, a fashion boutique, and an essential oils business… Well, I imagine that trading spices is a lot like selling essential oils.

It is crucial for us to not just accept what others say about what God wants us to do, but to seek God, read the Bible for ourselves, and dig deeper for understanding if necessary. Many commentaries mention the Proverbs 31 Woman's financial status, that she was an aristocrat. In other words, according to what's on the surface of this Proverb and the limited insight I found about it, I couldn't even afford to be like this woman. But there is more to this story. The truth is, women who are single, have no children, are full-time homemakers by choice, or have a lower income can all be like the Proverbs 31 Woman. We can all "have it all." No matter whether our lives match up with the scripture word for word, we don't necessarily have to live life exactly the way she did because her version of having it all doesn't have to be ours. Being a Proverbs 31 Woman does not mean doing everything that she did; instead, we learn the principles God wants to show us through her example.

So why even spend our time learning about her? I think God wants to use this woman to inspire us to be all that He has made us to be. Understanding the context of Proverbs 31 will help us properly receive the inspiration this passage has to offer and put it into practice to "have it all."

Chapter 2

One of the biggest questions I always had about the Proverbs 31 Woman was "Who is she?" I once heard a sermon preached about her that said she was Bathsheba, King Solomon's mother. The preacher said that Proverbs 31:10-31 was an ode to Bathsheba, and he used this Scripture to show us who we could become even if we thought we were insignificant or not good enough.

King Solomon of Israel was the son of King David. King David is famously known in the Bible as "the man after God's own heart," the one who killed Goliath with a sling shot on the first try when he was a teenager. He is also infamously known for dancing almost naked before the Ark of the Covenant because he was so excited that God's presence was going to be with the Israelite people. He was a warrior and the one God promised would be the great-great-great... grandfather of the Messiah, Jesus. But King David also had some huge scandal that cost the lives of some key people in his life.

I'm sad to say that I had to do my research before recounting this story for you. Not because I didn't know it, but because it's intense and certain details are unclear and I didn't want to speculate based on my own biases and experiences.

Here's what happened. One night, King David got out of his bed and saw a woman bathing. He thought she was attractive so he sent a messenger to go and get her. She went to him and he slept with her. She had just finished her menstrual cycle so she was fertile. Soon after, she had someone send him a message that she was pregnant. King David tried to cover it up and when his efforts failed, he essentially had her husband, a soldier, strategically placed on the front lines of a losing battle so that he would be killed. Then David married Bathsheba to further cover his sin. A prophet told him that God would spare his life because of his repentance, but among several consequences for his sin, the life of the child Bathsheba conceived would die (2 Samuel 12).

What saddens me here is that between the ambiguity of the biblical text and the political climate in America right now as of this writing, my first thought was, "Should I discuss whether this was consensual or did David rape Bathsheba?" I prefer to shy away from political debates, but for the sake of discussing Bathsheba as the Proverbs 31 woman I want to highlight this for a moment.

King David was supposed to be at war with his soldiers and he wasn't. He was supposed to be asleep and he wasn't. He already had more than one wife. He had the power to have his messengers find Bathsheba and *take* her to him. The Scriptures don't indicate whether she was "asked" by the messengers or David to have sex with him. It's unknown whether she had the freedom to say no, but when that is in question, consent is in question. Maybe the Scriptures don't highlight what happened in the bedroom — whether she was willing or enjoyed herself or resisted — because that wasn't the point. Before she stepped foot into that room, David had already abused his power. The he abused his power even further to cover up what he did — he made Bathsheba his wife as if he had never dishonored her or her husband. And God was angry about it.

Bathsheba had her husband and her child taken from her because of David's lack of self-control and on top of that she had to be stuck as his wife. But God did bless her with a son, Solomon, who would become the next King. King Solomon pleased God so much that God told him to ask for "whatever he wanted" (1 Kings 3). The young King Solomon asked for wisdom, and God was even more pleased with him. Solomon went on to write most of the Book of Proverbs, as well as all of Ecclesiastes and the Songs of Solomon.

When we speak of Proverbs 31, Christians are usually referring to verses 10 through 31, but verses

1 through 9 are believed to be written by the same person. In verse 1, the writer introduces himself as King Lemuel of Massa. In Jewish legend, Proverbs 31 is assumed to be written by Solomon because he wrote most of the proverbs. Some believed that Lemuel was a pen name for Solomon because Lemuel means "devoted to God" and Solomon was also called "Jedidiah" a name God gave him that means "loved by the LORD."

However, Proverbs 31 is, "an oracle his mother taught him" (verse 1). And since verses 1 through 31 are not separated in the original manuscripts, we can assume that King Lemuel's mom taught him about "The Proverbs 31 Woman" or "The Woman of Valor. This means that even if Lemuel was a pen name for King Solomon, The Woman of Valor couldn't be Bathsheba. But King Lemuel might not even be King Solomon. There is no evidence to support this, and the evidence that does exist about who King Lemuel is, suggests that he was a king from another country who converted to Judaism.

When I learned this, at first, I was disappointed. I had dreamed that a woman with a past like Bathsheba's could be a boss and icon like The Proverbs 31 Woman. I dreamed that Bathsheba had this Cinderella story in the end. I had that same hope for myself.

I have had my share of being a hot mess. Although I grew up in church, before I allowed Jesus to really be God in my life I had lost my virginity at 14. I was in some abusive relationships, and sexually promiscuous. I was almost a teenage mom. It was then, as a pregnant 16-year-old, that I realized I needed God yet didn't deserve Him. That's when the Cross became real to me. Jesus died on the Cross for me to be able to call out to Him to save me from my own sin when I needed help. Like David, I was able to repent to God after I messed up because God loved me. Like Bathsheba, I knew loss, because my teen pregnancy ended in miscarriage. But God completely turned my life around and I haven't been the same since.

That should have been enough of a Cinderella story and victory in my own eyes, yet I struggled to find my worth, recognize my identity, establish my career, and I have often looked to women such as The Proverbs 31 Woman, hoping to emulate something about them and be someone better than I am. I attached my shame to my success. I limited my worth to my works.

And that's how The Proverbs 31 Woman becomes an idol to us. An idol is anything we worship more than God. I wanted to be better more than I wanted God himself. It's a daily battle; to this day I can easily find myself using God in order to get to what I really want: to become better. Your story may be completely different from mine, but many of us women can relate to wanting to be someone other than who we are. I think that's why some Christian women obsess about the Proverbs 31 woman the way we do. I think it's why we gravitate towards any teaching we can find about her. We can be so dissatisfied with who and where we are now that we completely disregard the miracles God has already done to get us here. We worship this image of the "perfect" woman, hoping that she is someone who proves that we won't always be this way.

But she is not Bathsheba. In fact, The Proverbs 31 Woman is not even a real person.

The only real woman in Proverbs 31 is King Lemuel's mom in verse 1. Other than that, the woman King Lemuel's mom taught him about in verses 10 through 31 is the ideal woman she wants her son to marry. She sets this almost unattainable standard because she believes her son should choose the best wife. She lists one quality of this woman for each letter of the Hebrew alphabet. If you read it with this background in mind, it may even seem like she was just looking for something to say for each letter to make it that much harder for her son to settle down with somebody! Imagine her saying, "Son, if she doesn't work with wool and flax, she's probably not the one" (see Proverbs 31:13).

So we idolize an imaginary woman. We use her as our standard for everything we are not. That's not at all what God intended when he inspired the writers of His Word. There's nothing wrong with working hard, personal development, or seeing wisdom for how to live life well. What's wrong is our motive. I heard a pastor say that what we attribute worth to is what we worship and what we worship is where we find our worth. So if we find our worth in our story, accomplishments, how good our kids are, or what other people think of us, what does that say about our god? What does that say about God? I don't know about you, but I suck at being God and no one else is good enough to be God for me. I know that I need to continue to allow Him to do what only He does best. And the truth is, without Him I wouldn't be who I am today.

Before we see how The Proverbs 31 Woman is a godly example to us of how to have it all, we need to recognize what Proverbs 31 is not:

Proverbs 31 is not a formula for how to redeem your past.

God did not put this chapter in the Bible to give us a recipe for becoming successful women that would prove the world wrong for the way they hurt us, abused us, used us, and cast us aside.

God did not put this chapter in the Bible to show us how we could make our lives better than it was before.

God did not put this chapter in the Bible for us to say, "Well I don't have Bathsheba's past, so maybe I have a chance."

God did not put this chapter in the Bible for us to compare our lives to and see if we were good enough.

Proverbs 31 is not about how you can save or fix yourself by being organized, productive, or religious.

I'll go so far to say that Proverbs 31 is not even a chapter about how if we stay close to God we will become who we want to be.

We do not make our own Cinderella story. At the risk of being very corny and cliché and less than feminist, we needed a Prince to rescue us. That Prince — that King is Jesus. (Of course, men need Prince Jesus to rescue them too.)

I hate the popular saying, "You are enough," because it doesn't explain why or how. It's just, "you are enough," period. My question is, "I'm enough according to who? How I am enough?" If I'm the one who determines whether I am enough, I would be lying because I know myself at my worst. If I judge my "enough" based on what the world thinks of me, they might be biased because they see my best. But if God says I am enough, that's the only opinion that matters. And God never says we are enough.

Realizing this has freed me: I am not enough apart from Jesus. In fact, I'm too far gone without Him, the good I do cannot outweigh the bad I've done or will do. I can't do enough or be enough to get God to love me. But God still thinks I'm worth loving. He thought I was worth dying for before I ever lived. He died so that I wouldn't die separated from Him by my sin. He rose from the dead and His Spirit lives in me and changes me from the inside out. That's what makes me "enough." That's what gives me the permission to stop striving, to stop searching, to stop obsessing over what I lack. In Him I lack nothing.

The same is true for you. The Creator of the Universe thinks about you all the time. He made you in His image and He bragged about what a good job He did — He thinks you're wonderful! He wants to be with you and He moved from Heaven to Earth to do so. He saw how your shortcomings, your mistakes, and the ugly you try to hide would keep you separated from Him. So He made a way for you through Jesus' death and resurrection. He wants you to see Him as a Dad who loves to bless

His kids and give you the best life, and He wants you to enjoy it with Him in this life and the next, in Heaven. This is the Creator of the Universe, we're talking about! The Creator of time and space, who exists outside of them. The One who is the King of everything. And if you're His daughter, doesn't that mean you have it all?

But having God does not automatically mean you're living "the life" of the Proverbs 31 woman. If that was the case, this book wouldn't exist. There seems to be a disconnect between having God and seeing the life and dreams He give us manifest. Though we have it all, there seems to be such a struggle to get "there." But if religiously striving to do what The Proverbs 31 Woman did or become who she was isn't the answer, what is? We are going to dig even deeper into the purpose for these scriptures and how it can help us see the things God has for us come to fruition.

Chapter 3

One of my dreams was to be a dancer so, of course, when I was a teenager, I loved to dance and listen to music. I also liked to sing. I had all kinds of posters on my wall, from Michael Jackson — yes, even though I was a teen in the early 2000s — to Nelly, the rapper who always had a small bandaid on his face. And there was a time where I was in love with Chris Brown, the R&B singer — not to be confused with the gifted worship leader/songwriter at Elevation Church. I wanted to marry Chris Brown because he had beautiful caramel skin, was only about three years older than I, he could sing and dance, and was taller than I am. This could easily turn into a sermon about how man looks at the outward appearance, but God looks at the heart — I'll spare you. The height difference was a major requirement because I was already taller than my five-foot-three-inches petite mom by the time I finished 3rd grade, crying that I would never have a boyfriend. All the boys went through their growth spurts by high school, as she promised.

Now, knowing the kind of girl I was, I am paranoid that my kid will go through a boy-crazy stage like I did. She's only three and already practices kissing herself in the mirror, the way I did as a 2nd-grader, listening to Brittney Spears. (By the way, my dad once caught me during a mock make-out session between myself and dresser drawers, and I was mortified when he made me tell my mom what I was doing! I'm sure they had a quite a laugh when I went back into my room.) Then there's my husband who often jokes that he kissed all the girls in kindergarten except the one he actually liked. He became a Christian in 2nd grade and didn't date until college. He married his 3rd girlfriend, also known as yours truly, and lost his virginity on his wedding night. We are praying that our daughter takes after her Daddy in the "loving-Jesus-early" and "dating-wisely" departments. Pray along with me!

A major part of the drastically healthier changes that I made in my standards for a boyfriend was attending youth group. That is where I met my husband, after all. My youth pastor, Pastor Josh, would often tell us the story about how his wife, Tiffany, made a list of all the things she wanted in a husband and she gave it to God. That's how she knew PJ was the one. I remember being inspired to make a list of my own, constantly watering it down depending on who I was dating at the time. When I became friends with Roddy, I began to constantly add things to my list because I thought, "If there are guys out there like him, I'm going to ask God for more!" I didn't realize he was the best. I know — we're so cute!

I look forward to the day when my daughter and future kids start making their own lists (if marriage is part of God's plan for them) and submitting their lists to God. I hope to have the kind of relationships with them in which they would allow me to provide suggestions for their lists, as well as model for them, through my relationship with their dad, what kind of spouse they should pray for and aspire to be.

So even though I used to think that much of Proverbs 31 was unreasonably shallow and strict, I respect Mama Lemuel for giving her son such an in-depth list, one that He could memorize and pass down through generations. It is one that she compiled not to be uptight or discouraging, as if no one was good enough for her son. No, instead, it was written under the inspiration of the Holy Spirit, as with all Scripture — "God-breathed, [and] useful for teaching, rebuking, correcting, and training in righteousness, so that the servant of God may be thoroughly equipped for every good work" (2 Timothy 3:16-17). God would not have allowed it in our Bible if He Himself did not breath it into the writer. See 2 Peter 1:20-21.

To be clear, Proverbs 31 is not merely a guide to finding a wife. Though it may have been used as guidelines for King Lemuel to find a wife, the qualities mentioned in the passage are not just qualities for wives or moms. Can you imagine a husband searching for a wife who fits this description and not being an amazing man himself? Can you imagine a such a woman settling for a relationship with a man who knows how to find her, but has the audacity to not be able to show her why she would be better with him in her life? I can't imagine it! Side note, I think that being "unequally yoked" or having an unbalanced union is not limited to cases of Christians dating or marrying non-Christians, but mature Christians settling for immature Christians (2 Corinthians 6:14). If we read the verses before the famous "wife guide," Proverbs 31:1-9, we see that Mama Lemuel actually challenged her son to live to the highest standard as a king leading his people. She expected him to become the man who deserved the woman in the verses to follow.

So it makes perfect sense that Proverbs 31:10-31 is a passage that Jewish husbands and children would memorize and then recite to the mothers of the household as a Sabbath blessing. The passage calls all of us to a standard of godly excellence. Truly, Proverbs 31:10-31 includes wisdom for all women and men, at all stages of life — single, married, divorced, employed, homemaking full-time, and students, whether you dream of having a family or not — because it's not about the things the Proverbs 31 Woman did, it's about her character.

Regarding the purpose of the Book of Proverbs, Warren W. Wiersbe says, "The Book of Proverbs is about godly wisdom, how to get it and how to use it. It's about priorities and principles, not get-rich-quick schemes or success formulas. It tells you, not how to make a living, but how to be skillful in the lost art of making a life." (*Be Skillful*, p. 7.) The Proverbs 31 Woman is regarded as the epitome of wisdom. She is not wisdom personified, as you see in the beginning chapters of Proverbs where Lady Wisdom calls all of the young men to come learn from her. Instead, she is the picture of what we could be like in the fullness of wisdom that God has for us through the Holy Spirit. Through this passage, God shows us how to develop the kind of character that pleases him, fulfills us, and helps us to do all that He called us to do.

Because Proverbs 31:10-31 was written as an acrostic poem using the Hebrew alphabet as the first letters in each line, those of us who aren't fluent in reading Hebrew would naturally miss the main principles, having to read into what we think the important themes are. Ever since Adam and Eve ate the fruit in the garden of Eden, we have been naturally inclined to try to do things without God and find our own way to become "better." I think that's why many interpretations of Proverbs 31 have been skewed — they sometimes reflect the way we think we get better, not the writer's (or God's) intent. The danger in reading it that way is we make this passage works-based. We take God out of it completely because it becomes about us doing what we have to do to become like the Proverbs 31 Woman. Jesus fulfilled the law so that we could be free to live the life God intended. Therefore we have to look to Him in order for His word to be fulfilled in us. Yes, the Proverbs 31 Woman did good works and faith without works is dead (James 2:26), but God doesn't call us to do more, he calls us to remain in relationship with Him (John 15). That is how we become fruitful — that is how our lives and what we do reflects what God is doing in us, producing everything good. That is how we see change. I don't know about you, but I am so tired of starting healthy habits only to fail at them after a few weeks. I'm tired of trying to get better in the areas where I know I'm not obeying God, only to fall short again and again. I want lasting change, and that can only happen from the inside out — from becoming different, not just doing things differently. As we dive in to the Scripture as it was written originally, you will realize that we don't "do" to "become;" we "be" to "become." This is the part where I think you'll be mad at me. I think you're going to see how simple it is to "have it all" and you may think to yourself, "Really? That's it?"

In the following chapters, I am going to walk you through the principles of the Proverbs 31 Woman and "how to have it all." This is not based on what I think the verses mean in my English translations of the Bible. I won't group the Scriptures together into qualities that are not even mentioned, or strip them down to be so literal and religious that we think we need to start selling sashes at our local farmer's markets like in verse 24.

Instead, since this is an acrostic poem written in an ancient language, I did some research to find the Hebrew first words for each line of Proverbs 31:10-31. I assumed that it would be easy for someone to memorize an acrostic poem if they knew the first words. I imagined the young Jewish children who recited this poem to their mothers every Friday night. My daughter knows the English alphabet song because it's essentially an oral tradition that we have passed down to her. I imagined the Hebrew toddlers learning the first words of each line of Proverbs 31, understanding at least the general concepts of the poem until, as they heard it over and over, they learned each line, word for word. I wanted to see what the difference would be if we focused on the way it was written. It makes a world of difference, and I am so excited to share with you the insights I've learned that will help us grasp the way it applies to our lives today.

Most of the chapters in the next section will be a bit smaller (which is good because there are twenty two verses) and I include journaling questions and space to write your reflections, if you're into that sort of thing. I encourage you to savor each principle, returning to this book as a reminder, as you develop the character to become who God has called you to be. You will soon see the fruit of your character which will equip you to build the dreams God has given you.

Part II — The Secrets

I am so excited to breakdown Proverbs 31 with you. I hope it inspires you and helps you to read God's word in a new way. Here are some things you'll notice as I highlight the "first words" in each verse.

The Hebrew word and the pronunciation in English:
Because the Hebrew alphabet is made up of all consonant sounds and there are no vowels, we don't have a perfect transliteration, or change of letters, into English. I do my best based on my research to show you how the word is pronounced, plus the meaning that Bible translators give the word. I also show you other translations and synonyms of the word to help you better understand its meaning.

Exegesis:
Exegesis can be defined as "what the Scripture meant back then." I will show you more of the cultural and historical context of the verse.

Hermeneutics:
Hermeneutics is "what the Scripture means to us now." This is self-explanatory, but needs to be separated from the times and culture of when it was written so that we can receive what it's saying for us.

Journaling Questions:
Because I'll be doing a deep-dive with you, I wanted to give you some starting points for processing what you learn. This is completely optional. I am the kind of person who sometimes wants to journal and other times I want to speed read through it and come back to it later. Do not feel pressured to use the questions if you don't want to.

Chapter 4

אשת חיל

'eshet khayil — woman of valor
*An **accomplished woman** who can find?*
Her value is far beyond rubies.
Proverbs 31:10

The first words in the Proverbs 31 poem are
"woman of valor." The literal translation is "woman
strong." Valor can also be translated as,
"disciplined, army, strong, wealth, efficiency, etc."
This poem is not only an acrostic poem, it is an
heroic poem which means it is written to honor an
heroic person, usually a war hero. This poem was
written as if this woman has braved battles and been
victorious throughout her lifetime and her
accomplishments are worthy of commemoration.

Let's start with the very first word, "woman." It
could also be translated as "wife," as seen in other
English translations of the Bible, and wife is
certainly the context of the poem. But you don't
have to be a wife to be a woman, therefore, the
principles in this poem can apply to all of us.

There is no coincidence that "woman" is the
first word and not "valor." You can't "do" anything
to be woman, you just "are" a woman. It is your

41

assignment from before birth — before your father's sperm reached your mother's egg with two X chromosomes, God's plan for you was established and you were female. You were destined to be her. There was intention and purpose when God designed us. Therefore, you cannot be all that you were made to be without God. More so, you cannot have it all without embracing the destiny God gave you. The Proverbs 31 Woman was a woman who did not separate herself from her Creator, but embraced the purpose for which He designed her.

And she was strong in in her purpose — efficient in it, disciplined in it. The "valor" comes from seeking God to become all that He made us to be. She could be called "accomplished" because throughout her lifetime she succeeded in the things that mattered most. She knew what mattered most because of her connection to the Designer. She knew her God and could recall who He said she was and she did something about it.

This first verse asks the question, "Who can find her?" It is a rhetorical question, but she is not impossible to find, just difficult to find. She is like a rare gem and priceless.

Maybe she can't be found because women have been attacked from the beginning of time to forget who we are. Like Eve, Satan has tried to convince women that we are missing something and need to go get it. Maybe that is the reason books like this one attract us, because we want to be better than we are. We don't have it all so we need to go get it. Or worse, we feel something is missing but we accept that as normal and don't live the fullest life we were destined to live.

God called his creation good and that included Eve. Though she was equal to Adam, she was created with such strength that her help to him was comparable to God's help towards us. But she wasn't confident in what God told her or that what He said was what was best for her. Satan suggested to Eve that God was withholding something from her and that she was incomplete. So when she was tempted to go after something that, apart from God, could make her better, she took it. She ate from the fruit that she was forbidden to eat, willing to risk everything for a counterfeit version of the completeness that she didn't realize she already had in God. In her sin, she separated herself from Him and she was never the same. She lacked more than ever before and when she realized her mistake she hid.

"An accomplished woman who can find?" Maybe she is hard to find because she's hiding. She doesn't believe what God says about her and nothing she has tried to make her self better has worked for her. She is embarrassed, ashamed, living small, stuck in her sin.

Like Eve, many of us separate our design from what we do. We work out of our own limited strength instead of who God says we are. We strive to become an ideal like the Proverbs 31 woman but she becomes an idol to us because we won't rest in our relationships with God.

In order to have it all and become all that God created us to be, we have to let Him be God. We have to believe what He says about us.

Satan comes to steal, kill, and destroy. A woman of valor knows her worth, but Satan comes to steal that from her. She is grounded in God, but Satan comes to kill her by tempting her to do life separate from God. She is called to impact the world for God's glory, but Satan comes to destroy her legacy on earth and disrupt eternity.

But we will find her. No longer will we separate our deeds from our design. No longer will we define ourselves by what we do. No longer will we hide — we will bring our sin, our separation from God, into the light and allow him to cover us with His grace. We will accept Jesus' death and resurrection — allowing our old life to pass and accepting the new beginning, complete in Him. We will remember God's word when the enemy tries to tell us otherwise. We will find ourselves as we seek God and find Him. We will acknowledge His design with our lives. We will thrive in His purpose.

Have you been hiding? Striving? How can you accept God's design?

How can accepting what God says make you stronger?

When will you find time to read God's word? Will you believe it?

What has God said to you? About you? How can you live like it?

Chapter 5

בטח
batakh — trusts / has trusted
*Her husband's heart **trusts** in her,*
and he lacks nothing valuable.
Proverbs 31:11

The Proverbs 31 Woman was a wife, and
therefore her husband was one of the most
important people in her life. He not only knew her
best and her worst, but was also chosen by God to
protect her and provide for her (a unique part of his
design as a man). Adam failed in the Garden of
Eden when he watched his wife be tempted by the
serpent and didn't do anything to stop her. Whether
we are married or not, God places people in our
lives to safeguard us — holding us accountable to
what God has told us.

The first word in verse 12 is "has trusted." You
will notice that English translations of this Scripture
are often in present tense. This has more to do with
our modern culture where English proverbs are
written in present tense. Proverbs 31:10-29 is
written in past tense because it is an homage to a
woman's life.

So the first word here is "has trusted." This is significant because where the husband of the Proverbs 31 Woman trusts her, she finds freedom to do what is on her heart to do. He doesn't have to be concerned about whether she will make choices that ultimately sabotage her purpose. He can rest assured that whatever she does will be blessed.

This is different from believing in her. Anyone can believe in us but that doesn't make us trustworthy. People believe in us and we believe in them because of potential, not necessarily because of what we have already seen. Belief takes a level of faith, and faith is unnecessary when we can see what we're believing for.

The husband belief goes beyond what he can see — he doesn't just have faith in her, she has shown him that he can trust her. She has a track record with him. Therefore, he is able to release her to go after her dreams. He doesn't have to give her permission — though she submits herself to his permission knowing that God has given him a unique ability to protect her and that it doesn't hurt to have someone watching her back. More than that, though, he pushes her to do her things because she is in a healthy place. He doesn't have to worry about her and he knows that when she is thriving in her calling she blesses her household. The blessing to her household ripples throughout the world.

She has proven to him that her priorities are in order. She has put her relationship with God first, knowing that with God she has a 100% success rate — even her "failures" can be used for her good because she loves Him and is called according to His purpose. She knows who she is and the gifts God has given her. She has managed the little things and the key relationships in her life — she has nurtured her family and stewarded her home, finances, and everything else she has. She has delegated her weaknesses well. Maybe she hates cleaning the house, but she has created a system for keeping things in order, one that the kids can follow, or she has done so well with her gifts that her extra income enables the family to hire a housekeeper. Overall she has put first things first: God, her self-care, her husband, kids, and everything else — in that order.

We don't need people's permission to do what God has called us to do, but having the trust of the people who are called to safeguard us gives us the co-sign and extra confidence we sometimes need to be able do it without fear. The Proverbs 31 Woman was trustworthy because she trusted in God and surrounded herself with people who could help her stay on track with the vision God gave her. When we find our confidence in God, inviting Him and the people who know us best to guard us as we walk towards our dreams, we too are trustworthy. As we have that confidence that the people who know us best think us healthy enough to go to new levels and seasons of our calling, we have a confidence that gives them even more confidence in us. It is like a circle.

This verse goes on to say that the Proverbs 31 Woman's husband "lacks nothing of value." Other translations say he does not lack the "dividends" or he has "no need of spoil."

Sometimes when a business is getting started it needs investors, people who believe in the business and are willing to contribute funds to get it off the ground. The expectation is that the business will do well and the investors will get a return or profit on what they gave. It is a loan that they expect to pay off. In the same way, the husband's trust is like an investment in the Proverbs 31 Woman's destiny. And the Bible says he gets a return on his investment. He is not lacking — she hasn't robbed him by not being able to deliver what he expected. In fact, the word for "dividends" or "spoil" can also be translated as "plunder." It is as if in doing what God created her to do, she is like a warrior who, after defeating her enemy, takes everything they had — their silver, gold, everything valuable — and brings it back to her camp. Therefore, he lacked nothing of value. If that's not a powerful image, I don't know what is!

When we have confidence in God, and the confidence *of* God and the people who know us best, and we go to do what God has given us to do, we plunder the enemy on behalf of our family. We plunder the enemy and bring those blessings to the world. We are victorious and the people connected to us can be too.

And that is why I grouped the next verse together with verse 11:

גמלתהו

gemalathu — brings him good
*She **brings him good** and not harm
all the days of her life.*
Proverbs 31:12

The Hebrew word for "brings him good" is actually better translated as "repaid" or "rewarded." The husband has received the return on his investment. Not just today, but every day! This is just from the Proverbs 31 Woman being one who knows God and does what He wants her to do and, with accountability and support, she does it.

I am reminded of the Parable of the Talents, which can be found in the New Testament. In the Parable, the Master (who represents God) gives three servants (who represent us) a certain amount of money, called "talents," and tells them He'll be back. He gives to each servant according to what He

51

knows they can handle. The servant who receives five talents uses the five to get five more for his Master. The servant who receives two talents uses the two to get two more for his Master. The servant who has one talent buries it in the ground. When the Master returns He is pleased with the servants who multiplied their talents and He invites them into His Kingdom and Paradise. But the Master is not pleased with the servant who buried his talent. At the very least he could have put the money in the bank so that it would collect interest. So the Master takes the one talent away and casts that servant into the darkness where there is weeping and gnashing of teeth.

This parable shows God trusting us the way the Proverbs 31 Woman's husband trusted her. God expects us to bring Him a return on what He has invested in us. God not only believes in us, He trusts us enough to give us everything we have and He expects us to multiply it for His glory. When we forget that it belongs to Him, or we bury it, not making anything of what He has given us because we don't think it "matters" or compares to the people around us, we rob Him of the dividends He could have received. The good news is, there is still time. He gives us grace and patiently waits for us to prove Him right for trusting us. And He gives us the Holy Spirit to help us multiply what He has given us, despite fear. He puts people in our lives to check us when we are tempted to bury or forget the big picture: that we are part of God's economy, His story; that being with Him and loving for Him truly fulfills us as we bless the people in our lives and in the world.

When we multiply what God has given us, we plunder the enemy for God's glory. The Bible says we are God's reward (Deuteronomy 32:9), and He has no regrets.

Are you living a life worthy of the call of God (Ephesians 4:1)? We won't be perfect but we can expect to be perfect when Jesus returns for us and that's what we walk towards. And we live joyfully and thankfully, to see God's power at work through us doing exceedingly, abundantly above all that we could ask or think (Ephesians 3:20).

Is your trust first and foremost in God — in His word, His timing, His direction, etc.?

What "talents," resources, opportunities, and relationships has God given you to manage for Him?

Who in your life knows your ugly and your best and holds you accountable to God's best for you? (Hint: these are people who don't doubt you, but they are willing to check you.)

What would it look like if you were thriving in your calling? What would it look like for the people around you if you "plundered the enemy?"

Chapter 6

דרשה

darsha — selects

*She **selects** wool and flax*
and her hands work willingly.

Proverbs 31:13

"Selects" is the first word in verse 13, but it can be better translated as "sought out, inquired, investigated, or studied." In this verse we see the Proverbs 31 Woman seeking out the resources she needs to be able to use her gifts. In this case, one of her gifts is being able to make clothing, so she sought out materials to spin her own fabric. Thank God we don't need to do that in modern times. I have much respect for women all over the world who have mastered this work.

The verse also says that her hands work willingly. The word "willingly" is actually "delightfully" in Hebrew. Anyone can be willing — most people are willing to work, even if they hate their job, just because they need the money. Working delightfully is both a choice and a privilege. We can choose to make our work joyful or we can be blessed enough to do what we love. I think we are called to do both.

We won't always enjoy working, but we can find joy in it when we connect it to what God desires. The Bible tells us to delight in the Lord and He will give us the desires of our hearts (Psalm 37:4). Our joy in even the most difficult, stressful, painful, or mundane kinds of work comes from delighting in God.

We also experience "having it all" when we are able to use our passions and the things that bring us joy to bless others. Here is what King Solomon said in Ecclesiastes 2:24-26:

> "There is nothing better for people than to eat and drink, and to find enjoyment in their labor. This too, I perceived, is from the hand of God. For who can eat and who can have joy, apart from Him? For to the one who pleases Him, He gives wisdom, knowledge and joy, but to the sinner He gives the task of gathering and accumulating wealth to give it to one who pleases God. This also is only vapor and striving after the wind."

Because the Proverbs 31 woman delighted in God, she was able to use the things that she enjoyed to bless others for God's glory. She loved her work! King Solomon says, there is nothing better. We will see in the verses to follow that she was good at making fabric and sewing clothes, curtains, and bedspreads. Maybe the reason she became so good at it is she worked hard at what she enjoyed.

When we seek God and find joy in Him, He shows us how to take the things we love to do and do them well so that we can share His joy. He helps us gather the materials and knowledge we need to become good at what we do so that we can expand our impact. Oftentimes, our work, which can vary from season to season, is connected to what we're passionate about and helping people directly or indirectly. While we seek God to know what to do, we don't just seek God for His will, we seek Him knowing that He actually fulfills us. Our first and forever "calling" is to be in relationship with God and we bless people out of the overflowing fulfillment God has met in us.

What do you like to do?

What are you passionate about?

Do you find your fulfillment in God? If not, how can you start looking for your fulfillment in Him?

How can your fulfillment in God plus the things that you enjoy bless the world?

Chapter 7

היתה
hayta — was
*She **is** like merchant ships,
bringing her sustenance from afar.*
Proverbs 31:14

Because this poem is in past tense, the first word in verse 14 is "was" or "has been." The literal translation of the verse is "was like ships travel far bread." Hebrew is not an easy language to translate, to say the least.

Other meanings of the first word, "was," or "hayta" in Hebrew include, "has become," "has been established," "has abided," "has been done," and "has come to pass." The emphasis of the first word is who the Proverbs 31 Woman is because of where she has come from. She has a had a far journey to becoming the Proverbs 31 Woman. In life she brings her unique experiences to the table — her story, her past, her mistakes, her lessons, her growth. Ships traveling a far journey likely didn't always have smooth seas. In order to navigate the waters, you had to be a skilled sailor. This comes with learning over time and braving what was before her to become who she is.

Each of us has a story and a past that makes us who we are. We don't carry the shame, guilt, or sin that God nailed to the cross into our new life. However, with mistakes are lessons learned that have made us wise. With regrets, we have reordered our priorities in a way that we'll never have to go through those things again. From doing the right thing again and again, we have developed habits that made us more like the women God intended us to be. We have seen our good choices pay off. We have met people who have changed our lives for better or worse.

In order to reap all of the benefits of who we have been, we need to allow God's Word, the Bread of Life, to show us ourselves. We have to let God's Word hold a mirror to who we are and make us wise as we apply it to what has taken place (James 1:23-24). This is how you establish the woman that you are today. And tomorrow you will look back and be able to say that you have abided in God. you have remained in Him, you brought Him with you everywhere you went. Going forward you must take what God has taught you into every new place. In so doing, you bring that same sustenance to others. We see this in verse 15:

ותקם

vatakam — has risen

*She **rises** while it is still night*
and provides food for her household
and portions for her servant girls.

Proverbs 31:15

The Proverbs 31 Woman "has arisen," the first
word in verse 15. She has woken up before the
sunrise because she has a purpose for her day. She
needs all of the hours she can squeeze in to be able
to do what God has called her to do. She is strategic
about what she does at these wee hours of the
morning. She sets her servant girls up for success so
that they can have a productive day, allowing her to
do the things only she can do while they support her
in the things that anyone can do, the things she has
taught them to manage for her.

The word "arisen" can also be translated, "risen
oneself up." The Proverbs 31 Woman has answered
the call to leadership, she is self-motivated because
she knows God has called her. She does not belittle
the things God has called her to do, comparing
herself to the people around her. She knows that
everything she does is important to God and she is
determined to do everything for Him, with His help.
She has arisen knowing the importance of her work
and she has prioritized her time in a way to reflect

this, waking up before the kids or husband could "distract" her so that she could serve the women who are an extension of herself.

You may not have servants, and you may be in a season where waking before the sun is unrealistic, but I guarantee that you are called to be a leader. Being a leader doesn't mean that you're in the spotlight or that you're overseeing large amounts of people. On the contrary, it simply means having influence over people. Everyone who has a relationship with Jesus is called to influence others. At the very least we are to love them and introduce them to Jesus.

With your unique gifts, abilities, and personality, this can look very different from the way God wants to use your friends and family members to lead. Nonetheless, in order to have it all, you need to arise as the leader God has called you to be. You have to be intentional about becoming a woman who is worth following. When you combine who you have become (verse 14) with a commitment to wake up each day prioritizing your relationship with God and follow Him in the plans He has for you, and then bring that "sustenance" to others, you can maximize your influence as a leader.

You were born for it. Do not settle for less than becoming who God made you to be.

What are some experiences that you've had that have shaped who you are today? What is God's truth about those experiences?

What are some lessons and truths that you have learned that you have carried with you? What are you passing on to the people around you?

Are you allowing God to be your sustenance in every season? Will you be glad to look back and say, "I brought Him with me?"

What are you doing to "raise yourself up" to be who God has made you to be?

Chapter 8

זממה

zam'ma — considers

*She **considers** a field and buys it.*
From the fruit of her hands she plants a vineyard.
Proverbs 31:16

"Considers," the first word in verse 16 can be translated as "plots," which is usually a word with a negative connotation. A person who plots is often scheming to do something wrong, but such is not the case in this passage. We see the Proverbs 31 Woman literally shopping for a "plot" of land. "The fruit of her hands" refers to what she has gained and earned from her hard work — she is able to purchase this field with her own money and she plants a vineyard.

Sometimes "plotting" and thinking futuristically can cause us to worry. However, there is a difference between worrying and having vision. The difference is being aware of what you can control. If you are obsessing over something in the future that is out of your control today, that is worry. Jesus *commands* us not to worry. It is a waste of time.

On the other hand, dreaming about the future, plotting what you will do with the fruit of your hands that you earned today is wise. This can help

68

you determine how much you need to buy your proverbial "field."

Dreamers tend to feel a tug-of-war because they feel like they should be doing something. We sometimes cut our dreaming short and begin working on it before the dream has been plotted down to the minute details that would help us be successful. We do ourselves a disservice because when we get as far as the cutoff point of our dreams, we need to stop and dream again to know how to move forward. Sometimes we see that in cutting ourselves short we made decisions that would not have been made if we had the long-term vision before us.

So dream big. Dream until your dream scares you. Dream so big that after your dream has scared you, your mind can't process what comes next. Then start scheming. Get criminal-mastermind-intense about how to make it happen. (Don't plan a crime, but plan so well as if you desperately need to pull this off.) Invite God into your dreams to help you see how to make it happen. And when He gives you the first step, walk forward and trust him to show you the rest. In due time, the fruit of your hands will enable you to buy that field. And remember, when you thrive in God's purposes for you, the people connected to you thrive too.

What is your dream?

How can you invite God into your dream?

What is the first step to seeing your dream come to fruition?

Chapter 9

חגרה
khagra — girds
*She **girds** herself with strength
and invigorates her arms.*
Proverbs 31:17

The first word of Proverbs 31:17 is "has girded." This is referring to putting on a belt. In those times belts were used to either hold up a woman's tunic, or to hold tools for a worker or a sword for a soldier. Because this is an heroic poem, all illustrations apply perfectly. She is a woman, a worker, a warrior and therefore she needs the right equipment to carry out the different roles to which God calls her. In this verse, she equips herself with strength.

It would be foolish to think that "having it all" will come easily. Even with being connected to the King of the Universe, it's as if we have to catch up with what our spirit knows. We have old habits that try to hold us back, there are real circumstances that trip us up, people who want to discourage us, and then there is our enemy, Satan. He will not make it easy for us to "have it all" even though we have it all in Christ. He would rather see us struggle with trying to have it all while on earth so we won't have as great of an impact on eternity.

So we need to equip ourselves with strength. We read God's word because it is our sword, and the more that we know God's word, the more we can fight Satan as he tries to lie to us and distract us (Ephesians 6:10-18). We pray for God's grace to help us when we suffer because of circumstances, knowing that He makes us more mature through our trials so that we will "not lack anything," and, therefore, have it all (James 1:2-4). We receive the love that God freely gives us so that we can love the people around us, including the people who hurt us, knowing that Satan hates it when we pray for those who persecute us. We surround ourselves with people who love Jesus — the Church — because we know that we are all stronger together.

We also develop the unique strengths God has given us. The Proverbs 31 Woman strengthened her arms to be able to work the land she purchased and to make the clothing she would sell. In the same way, we not only strengthen ourselves spiritually, but through developing our skills, knowledge, and relationships we strengthen ourselves in every other way — mentally, emotionally, physically — for God's purposes.

What is one way that you can grow stronger
spiritually?

What is one what that you can grow stronger
mentally?

Emotionally?

Physically?

How can you continue to develop your unique
strengths/abilities? How will that make a difference
in what God has called you to do?

Chapter 10

טעמה

ta'ama — discerns

*She **discerns** that her business is good.*
Her lamp never goes out at night.
Proverbs 31:18

Proverbs 31:18 begins with the word "discerns," which is actually literally translated, "has tasted." "Taste" here is used figuratively to say that the Proverbs 31 Woman perceives that her business is good. In order for her to discern that her business is good, she has to have a standard of what good is and she must have goals. This comes from knowing her market, the quality of her products, etc.

This verse could be read to say her lamp doesn't go out at night because she is so successful that she doesn't need to put it out. However, it is more likely that excellence is so important to her that she stays up late to make sure that her business is good. She was so committed to excellence that she always stayed up late to do quality assurance.

For us the focus is not on staying up late, but on being able to discern whether our work is excellent. In order to do so, we need a standard, one that we can find when we stay connected to God's standard for us. In order to have "good taste" we have to know how to measure our "business." We can know this by reading God's word, having a godly mentor and looking to men and women who have gone before us, learning what *not* to do by watching people who have fallen, and gaining our own experience and measuring ourselves by our previous results.

Does your definition of success align with God's word? (Look up some Scriptures to be sure).

What does success look like for you in this season of your life?

Who are some people that you look up to as models for how to succeed in the things of God?

From whom or what circumstances have you learned how not to be successful?

Chapter 11

יָדֶיהָ
yadeyha — hands / palm
She **extends** her hands to the spindle
and her palm **grasps** the spinning wheel.
Proverbs 31:19

In Hebrew poetry, the hands are talked about in
twos to signify the right and left hand. We see a pair
of hands in verse 19 and another pair in verse 20 to
create parallelism, another Hebrew poetry
technique.

In verse 19, the Proverbs 31 Woman is working
with her hands, specifically extending one hand to
the spindle and grasping the spinning wheel with
the other hand. The Hebrew word for hands
specifically means "hold, strength, power, or
forearm." Often, to reflect there being a dominant
hand and a more "delicate" hand, we see hands in
Biblical poetry as being either strong and skilled or
soft and soothing. We see the contrast in the
following verse:

כפה
kapa — spreads / extends
*She **spreads** out her palms to the poor,*

80

*and **extends** her hands to the needy.*
Proverbs 31:20

Here the first word is another Hebrew word for "hand," but this time, her hands are showing their delicate side. Verse 20 shows us an open-handed woman who gives to people who are less fortunate than she. She knows to close her hands to work hard, in verse 19, so that she can open those same hands to be generous here in verse 20. She uses the gifts and skills God gave her to produce a blessing both for her family and for the world.

We are not here just to live comfortably and consume for ourselves until Jesus comes back for us. We are here to show others the compassion of Jesus — his mercy and grace through our outstretched arms and open hands. We are able to do this when we have worked hard for what our family needs and then sacrificially provide the needs of others through our excess. We are here to be loved by God, love Him, and love others. We put our hands to work, looking forward to being able to serve with these same hands. And the Bible says, it is more blessed to give than to receive (Acts 20:35). That's what it means to have it all.

What are some ways that you can manage your time, skills, and money so that you'll be able to bless people who are less fortunate?

How can you incorporate generosity into your everyday life?

How has God blessed you?

Chapter 12

לֹא-תִירָא
lotira — not afraid
She is **not afraid** of snow for her house,
for her whole household is clothed in scarlet wool.
Proverbs 31:21

"Unafraid" is the first word in verse 21. The
Proverbs 31 Woman has used what God has given
her to clothe and cover her family from the harsh
winter cold. She doesn't fear the elements or
circumstances coming her way; she is prepared.

We cover ourselves, our families, and the people
whose lives we are responsible to raise in scarlet
wool as well. It is no coincidence that wool comes
from the lamb and scarlet is the color of blood. We
cover our families with the Blood of Jesus — the
Lamb of God who was slain for our sins.

In the Book of Exodus in the Bible, Moses is
commanded by God to lead the Israelites in
observing the Passover. The Egyptians had long
held the Hebrew people captive and God had used
nine plagues to get the attention of Pharaoh whose
heart was hardened and would not release God's
people. God allowed Pharaoh to hold them a little
while longer so that He could display His power.

The tenth plague was the Plague of the Firstborn, in which the Angel of Death would come and strike the firstborn male of every household in Egypt. This was God's vengeance for the Egyptians' massacre of His children a generation before — a genocide that Moses was saved from in order to one day free His people. God commanded Moses to lead his people in sacrificing a spotless lamb, painting the blood of the lamb over the doorpost of their homes. The Angel of Death would pass over the homes in Egypt, see the blood of the lamb on the doors of the Hebrew homes, and pass over them, sparing the firstborn of Israel. When the Egyptian firstborns were found dead the following morning, including Pharaoh's firstborn, the Jews were set free from captivity. They didn't know that this exact event would symbolize the freedom of humankind from the bondage of sin.

Jesus is the Lamb of God who, by His blood shed on the Cross, has spared us from the curse of sin and death. He is our rescuer. So when you hear Christians "pleading the Blood of Jesus" they are claiming the freedom that God has given us — from sickness, from sin, for salvation (Isaiah 53:5).

Therefore we can be fearless when we are covered by the Blood of Jesus. We can pray for the Blood of Jesus to cover our homes and protect our family members. We can be unafraid because through Jesus even to die is gain (Philippians 1:21), we know where we are going when we close our eyes for the last time on earth — to Heaven to live forever. If death is the worst that could happen, nothing can terrify us.

What are you afraid of?

How can you submit those fears to God?

Chapter 13

מרבדים

marvadim — coverings

*She makes her own luxurious **coverings.***
Her clothing is fine linen and purple.
Proverbs 31:22

Verse 22 of Proverbs 31 starts with the word, "coverings." The word refers to tapestries and other household coverings such as that for a couch or bed. The verse also talks about the high-quality clothing that The Proverbs 31 Woman wears. Through her decor she sets an atmosphere in the room and through her dress, she brings a presence into it that is felt and contagious. She dresses as a wealthy aristocrat, in royal colors as if part of a Kingdom. This poem was, after all, originally written for King Lemuel to set the best standard for himself and his future wife.

As daughters of the King of the Universe we are called to represent Him. The Bible calls us ambassadors (2 Corinthians 5:20). Therefore, the places where we dwell and establish ourselves are like embassies. Because we are citizens of Heaven (Philippians 3:20), everywhere we go we bring Heaven with us. When we walk into a room, clothed in compassion, kindness, humility, etc. (Colossians 3:12), we should see something shift because God is with us. We wear what represents Christ, and throw off anything that would confuse people from seeing Jesus in us. We are, after all temples of the Holy Spirit (2 Corinthians 6:16). We are the Body of Christ.

We don't neglect the physical things that allow us to be ambassadors for Christ. We practice self-care, we take pride in our appearance and care for the spaces in which we live and work because God uses practical things to speak to people spiritually. We nurture ourselves so that we can continue to be energized in loving people. We also create hospitable areas for people to visit a slice of Heaven when they are with us.

Our domain away from our heavenly home should be a place where people can sense the presence of God in the atmosphere. Everywhere we walk should be holy ground, therefore our embassy is wherever we go. An embassy is like having part of the country on foreign land — wherever we are is God's territory. Therefore we live with authority, knowing that we have the stamp of approval from our King. We prepare ourselves to grant asylum — refuge and rescue — to those who are looking to turn to God and be part of His Kingdom. That is our mission.

What are some ways that you can clothe yourself spiritually to look like an ambassador for Jesus? (Hint: Clothing spiritually is an inward work.)

What are some ways that you can set the atmosphere wherever you go so that people experience a slice of Heaven?

What are some practical things you can do for your self-care or home management routine to be able to be hospitable with people?

Chapter 14

נודע

noda — respected

*Her husband is **respected** at the city gates,*
when he sits among the elders of the land.
Proverbs 31:23

In verse 23 of Proverbs 31, the husband seems
to be the focus. The first word is "has been
respected," which can also be translated, "has been
known, has been recognized, has been well-known,
has been skillful." Because the husband is likely a
man who is equally matched to his wife in valor, we
can assume that he is respectable on his own.
However, because this is a poem about her, we can
also assume that part of the reason he is well-known
is because of his wife. She is a woman who honors
him and respects him when no one else sees him.
Maybe she knew him when he was at the bottom of
the ranks and supported him to the top. Maybe in
her conversations with the merchants, who we'll see
in the next verses, she talked him up — not because
he needed her to make him look good, but because
he was good — and maybe the merchants listened
because she herself had a good reputation. Proverbs
12:4 says, "A noble wife is the crown of her
husband, but the wife who acts shamefully is like
rottenness in his bones." Because of her character

he was able to trust her (as in Proverbs 31:11), and we see here one of the benefits of his support is that it's mutual.

In order to be women who have it all, we must be willing to honor, support, and celebrate others — in private and in public. It is so easy to be jealous of women who are doing "better" than we are. It is so easy to put our husbands down for the one annoying thing they did instead of celebrating the fact that they are present in the lives of their kids, even if they keep leaving socks lying around the house. It is so easy to focus on the negative and, worse, talk badly about people when they aren't around. It often comes from our own pride, thinking we are better or deserve better and therefore can compare ourselves to them.

The Proverbs 31 Woman did not have time for all of that nonsense. She was committed to building a legacy for God's glory and that legacy included her whole family. Therefore, helping her life partner make major career moves was important to her. She realized that for her family to maximize their potential, they had to be a team. That doesn't mean she pushed or pulled him along to be who she wanted him to be. Rather, she did her part in encouraging him (and you know she was definitely praying for him) in the things she saw God doing in his life.

We can do the same for anyone we are connected to; not in a manipulative way, just by seeing the good and saying what we see. When we are quick to give shout-outs and hi-fives to others on their accomplishments (big or small) and their godly character, God honors us too. (We'll see this towards the end of the poem.)

How are you doing with celebrating the people in your life?

How can you become more aware of the good in people?

Is there anyone that you're jealous of? How can you turn that jealously into respect and inspiration?

Who are some people that you will intentionally celebrate privately and publicly?

Chapter 15

סדין
sadin — linen
*She makes **linen** garments and sells them*
and supplies sashes to the merchants.
Proverbs 31:24

It is a little odd that the first word in verse 24 of
Proverbs 31 is "linen." "Linen" refers to the sashes
that she would sell to the merchants. A sash was
worn as a belt. Most men of those times would wear
a tunic with a sash tied around it to keep everything
in place and a coat over everything. The Proverbs
31 Woman was able to make something that could
bring in a profit while at the same time meeting a
necessity among the business people in her town,
who may or may not have been Jewish. She figured
out what people needed and determined how her
skills could be used to meet that need. She wasn't
afraid to ask for compensation because she provided
something valuable to people.

Our skills can be used to help people by just
meeting a need for them. When people are willing
to compensate us for our work, it means that we
blessed them. The Proverbs 31 Woman was so good
at her craft that she was able to make it a business.
Not all of us are called to be business people but we

are called to be about our Father's business. When we do anything, it is a reflection of what God has given us. So we must carry ourselves as people who not only want to use our skills, but be excellent in them, serving people with such value that if they paid us, it wouldn't even compare to how much we're really worth.

Whether we choose to be compensated or not is between each of us individually and God. Making money by using the gifts God has given you to bless people is not immoral — it just proves that you are a blessing. Not making money from the way you serve people does not necessarily mean you're better than someone who makes a living from their work — it just means you probably have the flexibility in your budget to be able to do so. Sometimes the more we earn, the more we can bless our families and communities and have influence in a way that allows us to point more people to Jesus.

The Proverbs 31 Woman did not separate the secular from the sacred. She knew that as God's child using God's gifts to serve people, she was doing holy work, no matter whether she made a lot of money or served people with a different faith than hers. She treated it all as God's work, and therefore she did her best.

How can God use you, with the skills you have today, to serve the people in your community? What do you have to offer them?

In what areas have you been separating the secular (non-religious) from the sacred (religious)? How can you bring the sacred into everything you do?

Chapter 16

עוז-והדר

ozvehadar — strength and dignity
Strength and dignity *are her clothing,*
and she laughs at the days to come.
Proverbs 31:25

Proverbs 31:25 combines "strength" and
"dignity" into one word to start the verse. The
Proverbs 31 Woman is seen as someone who is
strong and honorable. These are inward qualities
she possesses so greatly that they can be seen when
people look at her. These qualities are what keep her
form being worried about what the future may
bring. She is able to laugh at the days to come
because she is tough enough to handle it. This
strength is, of course, from God. The Bible tells us
that those who hope in the Lord will never be put to
shame (Romans 10:11). The Proverbs 31 Woman
has seen this to be true. God has been constant and
faithful. He has brought her joy in difficult seasons
and kept her through them. That joy has become her
strength (Nehemiah 8:10). So she can mock the
days to come because she knows that with Him, she
can handle it. More than that, she knows Who holds
her future.

There is too much purpose on each of our lives today to be stressed about what is coming tomorrow. If we commit ourselves to Jesus and remember that we did so, we can go about the things we have been called to do in this season with strength and dignity. We don't need to freak out because we know that God is in control. It's not just a cute saying, it's one that releases us from trying to make everything work together.

There are certain things we would never see a diva do. Usually "divas" cannot do certain trivial things because they feel it is "beneath them." The Proverbs 31 Woman was not a diva in her attitude (you'll see in following verses that she was kind), but she had the dignity to be able to laugh at the days to come because the worries of tomorrow were beneath her.

Stressing about tomorrow is also beneath us. All things are under Jesus' feet (Ephesians 1:22). If we are His Body, then we have to be aware that the things the things with which the enemy comes against us are beneath us. We must be clothed in dignity, knowing that we are above letting him mess with us and our families and our calling. We may go through difficult times, but we know that God is on our side and he has already won — therefore, we win too! The Proverbs 31 Woman knew she was a winner — not because of her own personal pride, but all for God's glory. When we walk in this peace,

it can be seen from the inside out, and remember —
it's contagious.

What are some things that are "beneath you" that
you are allowing to disrupt your peace? (Use
Scripture to be sure.)

How will you remind yourself that you are
victorious in Jesus?

Chapter 17

פיה

piha — mouth

*She opens her **mouth** with wisdom—*
a lesson of kindness is on her tongue.

Proverbs 31:26

The first word in Proverbs 31:26 is "mouth." We see here that though some things were "beneath her" (see the last chapter), the Proverbs 31 Woman spoke with wisdom and kindness. The word "mouth" here is used to symbolize the way she talked.

The Proverbs 31 Woman's mouth opened with wisdom. The poetic imagery here suggests that wisdom is the key to unlocking her words. This can mean a few things. It could mean that she literally only opened her mouth to say wise things. It is likely that she was not a woman of many words and used her words wisely. This verse can also mean that when she had something wise to say she opened her mouth. She would not keep her wisdom to herself — she shared it with others. She wouldn't hide and wait for permission to speak. She chose to speak the truth with boldness so that others could benefit from it.

We also see that in this verse kindness is on her tongue, another figure of speech. In English a synonym for "tongue" is "language," (i.e. "her native tongue"). Kindness is the Proverbs 31 Woman's primary language. Though she is a wise woman and probably knows better than most people, she does not speak her truth harshly, but with love.

In the same way, we must practice wisdom when we speak. Are there times when we can listen better so that we are able to answer in a way that is most beneficial for the people with whom we are conversing? Are there times when we should be speaking up because God put something on our heart to share with others, but instead we are shying away and keeping it to ourselves? We must ask God for both the wisdom and boldness to open our mouths.

We must also learn the language of kindness and become fluent. This can be difficult. Speaking differently begins with thinking differently, and so often we don't even speak kindly to ourselves in our thoughts. We need to learn to hear God's voice so that we know what lovingkindness sounds like. Then we need to practice thinking kind thoughts about ourselves and others. We learn to hear God's voice by spending time with Him in His word and in prayer. Then as our thoughts change, so will our speech.

Does your mouth open with wisdom?

How can you become more fluent in "kindness" today?

Chapter 18

צוֹפִיָּה

tsofiya — watches

*She **watches** over the affairs of her household,
and does not eat the bread of idleness.*
Proverbs 31:27

Verse 27 begins with the word "has watched."
The Proverbs 31 Woman "has observed," "has
watched closely," and even "spied" on her
household affairs. She has been tracking the
patterns that have been taking place within her
home and she has acted accordingly. She has been
aware of the direction in which things were headed.
She has watched to be sure that the things that took
place in her home were in line with the vision she
and her husband had set, with God's help.

Practically speaking, the Proverbs 31 Woman is
making sure that her home has everything they
need. "Eating the bread of idleness" could refer to
receiving handouts or charity, but it is more likely
that the verse is saying she has worked hard to make
sure that her home was well stocked with
necessities.

As managers of God's property we must work hard to care for all of it. In order to avoid ending up a place where we need to receive handouts, we keep track of what we have. Spiritually, we need God's discernment to know what is needed in our homes and at work. We can use God's word to see areas where we are lacking and do something about it. We can pray for God to show us areas that need maintenance before they break down (i.e. mental health, relationships, the lives of our children, and decision-making).

When we are aware of our own health and the health of our households and businesses, we can know what to do to become better. We can know when and how to slow down, and we can know if we're ready to push ourselves a little harder. Regardless of what happens around us, the healthier we are, the more we experience the "life to the fullest" that God desires for us.

How can you grow in self-awareness?

What are some areas of your life that can be healthier? Allow God to give you the steps to work on those areas.

How are you keeping track of the health of your home, business, etc.

Chapter 19

קָמוּ

kamu — risen

*Her children **arise** and bless her,*
her husband also praises her:
Proverbs 31:28

"Risen" is the first word in Proverbs 31:28. The Proverbs 31 Woman has raised a family and now they have risen up to bless her. Because this poem is about a woman's life, we see that these are her adult children who are grateful for the lessons she has taught them by the way she lived her life.

Verse 29 shows us what exactly they said to her:

רבות

rabot banot — many daughters

*"**Many daughters** have excelled,*
but you surpass them all."
Proverbs 31:29

The first words in verse 29 are "many daughters." Her children and her husband are the people who are closest to her and yet they are still able to bless her. They are able to say that she is the most excellent of all noble women — even though they know her "dark side." That is a huge honor!

The Proverbs 31 Woman has sought God and did what He wanted her to do. She was creative, she loved people, and she was wise. These are the things that her family saw and they praise her for it.

When we are being who we need to be, we don't need to compare ourselves to anyone else because no one can be who we are. You are the best you and I am the best me. We will surpass the many who "do" excellent things by actually excelling in who God calls each of us to be.

Are you being the best you?

What do the people who know you best (the real you) say about you?

How can you excel at being yourself?

Chapter 20

שֶׁקֶר
sheker — deceitful / lies
*Charm is **deceitful** and beauty is vain,*
but a woman who fears Adonai will be praised.
Proverbs 31:30

The end of this poem switches to present tense.
At this point, the poet encourages the people of
modern times to honor the women of valor in their
lives. This is where the Sabbath ritual of the
husbands and children reciting this poem to the
mother of the house really comes to life.

Verse 30 begins with the word "lies." It's a little
ominous and it's the most negative first word in this
poem, but it continues the thoughts of the verse
before. Trying to impress people is like lying — it's
fake and misleading and doesn't last — but a
woman who reveres God will be praised.

This verse discourages from trying to be
someone that we are not. We don't need to try to
make people like us more or think highly of us
based on who we are on the inside. Instead, we
should just put God first. We should just worship
Him above all else and live to obey Him. He
already approves of us if we have accepted the gift

of salvation through Jesus. Having faith in Him makes it easy to please Him through obedience, especially with the Holy Spirit helping us. And if we fear God, we will be praised.

I used to think it would be weird to be praised until I understood the following and final verse of Proverbs 31:

תנו-לה
tenula — give
Give *her the fruit of her hands.*
Let her deeds be her praise at the gates.
Proverbs 31:31

The first word here is "give." The expression "give her the fruit of her hands" means "give her what she is due." Give her what she deserves. She worked for it, let us honor her. This is a command to us in the present day.

Then we see the Proverbs 31 Woman being praised by her works. She has privately used her life to worship God in such a way that she has earned the right to be praised in public.

If we are God's works and we praise Him, what happens when the works of God's works praise? When we are praised for the things that we have done, it is as if God is being praised because He is the One who made us. We are His workmanship, created to do good works which He has prepared for us in advance (Ephesians 2:10).

So then, let us praise God through our works so that our works will bring even more praise to God. Let us become praiseworthy so that we can point the glory back to Him.

Are you living your life in a way that the things you do bring praise to God?

Epilogue

So we took a look at the secrets of the Proverbs 31 Woman and almost all of it had to do with her character and her relationship with God. Is that really the secret to having it all? Yes.

God has plans for us that are unfathomable. They are plans to prosper us, not to harm us — plans to give us a future and a hope (Jeremiah 29:11). He has everything and He loved us so much He did not even spare His Son's life in order that we would be guaranteed eternity with Him. Do you think He would withhold any good thing from you? (See Romans 8:31-32.)

But He doesn't force Himself on us. All of the things God wants to give us and the plans He wants us to be apart of, we need to accept. It is a daily journey but each day we can have it all because we have Him.

So how do you begin to see the "all" in your life? Where should you begin?

1. Begin with God. Stop trying to figure things out on your own. He wants to help you. His dreams for you are better than the dreams you have for yourself. Seek God first. Everything else comes

along with knowing God. Then you will find freedom to walk in whatever makes sense to you to do because your heart is so in tune with God's desires. He will fulfill you even when what's on the outside doesn't look like "having it all." In the seasons where things looks "poopy," the joy of the Lord will be your strength.

2. Develop yourself. Ask God to help you to grow into the woman that He design you to be. Do not settle for anything less than who He says you are. The Proverbs 31 Woman is famous because she knew who she was in God, she loved Him, and she used everything He gave her for His glory. In doing so, she was able to be a woman of valor and accomplish so much in her lifetime. Remember that a life like hers takes a lifetime to live. There are seasons. Savor them. Number your days.

3. Establish your family. If you have a spouse, put your relationship with him first — that will set the order in your home so that you can raise kids on a stable family foundation, one that will last when they leave the nest. Invest in your kids. Model for them what it looks like to love Jesus and teach them about Him whenever you get the opportunity. He will help you figure out the rest. If you do not have a family yet, live your life in such a way that when your family

comes along, you will be healthy enough to prioritize them while doing whatever God is calling you to do apart from your family identity. Your family will be one of the most important opportunities for you to use your gifts for God's glory, but remember that you are more than a mom or wife — you are God's daughter first. If you don't desire to have a family, disregard this part.

4. Do well with what you have. You have resources, skills, connections, and opportunities that are unique to you. You are here in this time for a reason — don't take anything for granted. Work hard, rest well, be creative, love people. Use everything He has given you. God doesn't give us what we have just to make us feel good about ourselves — He expects us to multiply it because He is expecting a return on His investment. You will find that waiting for Jesus' return is fulfilling while you not only have a relationship with Him but LIVE for Him — serving, giving, doing, blessing, enjoying, sharing. Ask God for His vision so that as you seek Him and seek to live for Him, you can have direction on how to move every day.

5. Dream with God. Let Him give you dreams that scare you. And as they draw closer to accomplishment, dream even bigger!

The truth is when you have God you have everything! The Bible says He is our portion and reward (Psalm 73:26). Paul counted everything as dung in comparison to knowing Christ (Philippians 3:8). There's something to it — Jesus is everything. When you have Him, you have it ALL and then some. Having it all doesn't just take a lifetime — it is a mindset of knowing that because you have Christ, you have it all, and that makes the journey that much more incredible. You have priority level VIP access to the King of the Universe. You have it all. As you grow in relationship with Him, you will see "all" continue to come to fruition until eternity.

Made in the USA
Coppell, TX
09 May 2021